The RUSTIC WEDDING Handbook

MAGGIE LORD

*

PRINCIPAL PHOTOGRAPHY BY MAGGIE CARSON ROMANO

GIBBS SMITH
TO ENRICH AND INSPIRE HUMANKIND

First Edition
18 17 16 15 14   5 4 3 2 1

Text © 2014 Maggie Lord
Photographs © 2014 Maggie Carson Romano
except as noted on page 159

Published by
Gibbs Smith
P.O. Box 667
Layton, Utah 84041
1.800.835.4993 orders
www.gibbs-smith.com

Designed by Rita Sowins / Sowins Design
Printed and bound in China

Gibbs Smith books are printed on either recycled, 100%
post-consumer waste, FSC-certified papers or on paper
produced from sustainable PEFC-certified forest/
controlled wood source. Learn more at www.pefc.org.

Library of Congress Cataloging-in-Publication Data

Lord, Maggie.
The rustic wedding handbook / Maggie Lord ; principal
photography by Maggie Carson Romano.
— First edition.
pages cm
ISBN 978-1-4236-3461-4
1. Weddings—Planning. 2. Wedding
decorations. 3. Handicraft. I. Title.
HQ745.L673 2014
392.5—dc23
2013050686

For Our Mothers

CONTENTS

* ACKNOWLEDGMENTS *

I never believed that I would be the author of one book, let alone three. Along this journey I have been so blessed to work with a list of very special, talented, influential and creative people who have added to this project and to the Rustic Wedding Chic company as a whole. A big thank-you to Hollie Keith and the team at Gibbs Smith, Publisher for making yet another beautiful book and for helping to expand the world of Rustic Wedding Chic. To Maggie Carson Romano for jumping into this project with both feet and opening up my world to so many beautiful ideas and for being just the most wonderful friend. A big thanks also to Charlie Panian for assisting on this project in a variety of forms. I could not and would not have wanted to do our craft projects with anyone other than the women of Rambling House Events. Endless thanks are in order to Kate McKenna who is one of the most talented women I know. To my family for their unending support. To my son, Jack, and husband, Jon, who are my everyday inspiration.

—MAGGIE LORD

First I must thank my loving family for always challenging me and for showing endless support of my many pursuits. Thank you to Jurow, my best friend and handsome other half, for sharing me with this project throughout this last year while providing constant support and encourage-ment. And a huge thank-you to Charlie for lending us your many strengths, and for acquiring my iron goose at the Raleigh Flea Market, whom I love dearly. Lastly, my deepest gratitude goes to Maggie for approaching me with this project and for being the motivating and organizational force that made this book what it is. I am so thankful for the constant enthusiasm and focus you showed throughout our collaboration. I love you all so much.

—MAGGIE CARSON ROMANO

INTRODUCTION

THE MOMENT YOU SAY YES, THE WEDDING-DAY DREAM BEGINS TO TAKE SHAPE. Look closely—what do you see in this vision? Is it fully formed or filled with possibility? Will you hear the crunch of autumn leaves underfoot as you walk down the aisle? Will you stand together, hand in hand, in the fresh country air to promise "till death do us part?" Will cherished guests sip champagne from crystal coupes and dance with you under the glow of lantern light? A rustic wedding is all of this and more. It's the peace of putting your personal touch on this momentous event. It's the thrill of beautiful details that you'll never forget. It's the joy of marrying your best friend, surrounded by love, in a place that captivates your spirit. Welcome to your rustic wedding day.

After completing my first two books, *Rustic Wedding Chic* and *Barn Weddings,* it seemed only natural that my next book project should bring all the elements of planning a rustic wedding together in one place. After all, I do spend my entire workday researching ideas, writing tips, and showcasing beautiful real weddings on the Rustic Wedding Chic blog.

Here I have set out to compile all the information and knowledge I have gathered since starting the blog back in 2009. From the very beginning, I focused on sharing ideas and resources that I felt were missing for rustic brides to bring their rustic wedding goals to fruition.

I initially created the Rustic Wedding Chic blog when I was planning my own lakeside wedding in the small midwestern town where my family summers. After searching in countless wedding magazines, wedding sites and books, I felt there was a huge lack of inspiration and ideas for brides like me who are planning a rustic yet chic wedding day. Hoping to make the process easier for other brides, I created the blog to act as a daily muse and a place to find not only inspiration and ideas but also real resources and vendors who could help the bride-to-be in creating her dream rustic affair.

After blogging about hundreds of real weddings and studying thousands of beautiful wedding images, I know one thing for a fact: every wedding starts with the seed of an idea, an inspiration. Maybe it's blissful childhood memories of summers at the lake or the pure romance of tying the knot in a wide-open country field. Perhaps it's as simple as celebrating with all your loved ones together in your very own home. It's just this type of memory or mood that can serve as the perfect jumping-off point for couples as they begin to build their ideal day. Like an artist painting a picture or a chef creating a meal, the wedding planning process is a creative one. Your wedding's inspiration will be both a springboard for the project and a touchstone to return to as this vision adapts to the many diverse elements that will comprise your rustic wedding day.

The beauty of a rustic wedding is its versatility and all of the creativity that it brings about. Drawing on the wonderful ambiance of a natural, rustic setting and expressing your own personal style in a less traditional fashion is an exciting opportunity for couples to say "I do" in a way that is perfectly unique to them.

As your rustic wedding style begins to take shape, bringing this inspiration to life will require those special pieces that will make the day feel as personalized as possible. When hunting for these unexpected items, the ones that will make your day one hundred percent unique to you and your significant other, you may need to think outside the box. There was a time not so long ago

when the words "flea market" and "wedding" were about as far away from one another as they could get. Today, it is entirely acceptable and, as you'll see here, encouraged for couples to cull from a wide variety of sources for extraordinary wedding day design elements.

Join me here as I hit the flea market in Raleigh, North Carolina, shop the racks at local stores, and seek out the finest online vendors to showcase the best ways of hunting and gathering those wonderful personal expressions of your wedding style. The only limit to finding exactly what you want for your wedding day is your imagination. But for now, let's start at the beginning . . .

CHAPTER ONE

GETTING STARTED

THE JOY AND EXCITEMENT THAT COMES WITH GETTING ENGAGED IS UNLIKE ANY OTHER MOMENT IN LIFE. It's filled with all the promise of a new journey together and the endless possibilities of what your wedding day will be. But where to start? For many couples this early planning phase is the most difficult. Even for the most serious wedding aficionados, the reality of taking those first steps can be overwhelming.

I often receive emails from couples via the "Ask Maggie" section of the Rustic Wedding Chic blog about the best way to start the planning process. I always suggest that couples break this first phase of planning into three key decisions: when, where and who; in other words, The Date, The Venue and The Crowd. By addressing these fundamental areas right off the bat, you can start to build out the rest of your wedding day vision. Other aspects of the wedding such as style, decorations, food and logistical considerations (think bathrooms and parking) will fall into place much more easily.

ADDING TREES OR TALL PLANTS TO A BARN SPACE CAN HELP TO MAKE THE SPACE FEEL MORE INTIMATE AND ELIMINATES THE CAVERNOUS FEEL.

WHEN: THE DATE

YOU CAN BE SURE THAT ONCE YOU GET ENGAGED, family and friends will start to ask when to expect the big day. Whether it's a short engagement or a long one, sooner or later you have to select a date. This is often easier said than done, so to make the decision more manageable, I've broken it down into four steps.

STEP 1: SELECT A SEASON—By honing in on a season, it becomes instantly easier to identify key style elements and rule out others. Color palettes, floral design and even menu choices become less overwhelming to consider within the parameters of your chosen season. Keep in mind that late spring and early summer are the most popular seasons for weddings. You're already making progress!

STEP 2: SELECT A MONTH—You've chosen a season; now choose your preferred month. Take a moment to cross-reference birth dates, holidays and other notables; after all, you'll be celebrating anniversaries on this date, too.

STEP 3: SELECT A DATE—To account for hectic schedules on both sides of the aisle, offer three potential dates to your family and wedding party. This will assist in finding the date that works best for the key players you need in attendance.

STEP 4: INQUIRE WITH VENDORS—Whether you are hoping to host your wedding in an established venue or want to throw a more casual, backyard-style wedding, start to reach out to venues and vendors. The earlier you can check availability, the better, especially when it comes to popular venues or the busy summer and fall months. Some venues book events up to two years out, so if you have a specific venue in mind, you might want to inquire as soon as possible.

WHERE: THE VENUE

THE SKY IS THE LIMIT WHEN IT COMES TO SELECTING A VENUE FOR YOUR WEDDING. You may already be picturing an old dairy barn, a vineyard or an urban loft, but keep an open mind and you will find a venue that works for you, your style and your budget.

I have had the pleasure of reviewing thousands of beautiful and unique rustic venues from around the country on the Rustic Wedding Guide section of the blog. Each venue is so different—with its own personality, opportunities and challenges. How to decide? Consider these insights from the many venues, vendors and real couples who have written to the blog to share their experiences with us.

Start with a (long) list of possible venues that have some or all of the qualities you are thinking about. For example, an outdoor ceremony location, a barn, views, water, horses and fields—whatever is important to you as a couple. Regardless of your venue preference, even if it is as

IF PLANNING AN EVENING WEDDING IN A BARN SPACE, MAKE SURE YOU HAVE
AMPLE LIGHTING FOR GUESTS TO SEE AND NAVIGATE THE LANDSCAPE.

informal as a friend's backyard, there are several important factors to take into account before committing. Do your homework: find out if the venues you like will be available on or near your chosen date and if they'll be able to accommodate your budget and the size of your wedding.

You will be able to cross some off the list based on those initial key factors. Now with a much shorter list, here comes the fun part . . . setting up appointments to visit. Never make a decision based just on what you see or read online. While that is a great place to start for an overview of the property, their philosophy and what they have to offer, an in-person visit is worth making time for. Taking time to visit in person your short-listed venues will be enormously helpful in finding the right location.

Make an appointment with the owners or wedding coordinator to learn as much as possible while you are there. Certainly wander around by yourselves, but make sure to meet with the management. Getting a feel for them and the type of establishment they run is a very important step. You'll be able to cross some venues off your list with ease. It may not look the way you had imagined or the staff may not be as hands-on (or hands-off) as you need them to be. But this will help you narrow the field to two or three solid prospects. While many discourage a drop-in visit, it doesn't hurt to stop by one more time to be sure you are still in love with it and it deserves to be on the short list.

Next, it's time to get down to brass tacks with each of your venue finalists. Making the choice can be tough, but in the end you will have your venue and the fun of planning can truly begin! Don't hesitate to ask the hard questions as you weigh your options. A few examples are listed below and on the next several pages.

* Hours *

Make sure to take all the phases of your wedding day into account when discussing time frames and hours with your venue, including preparation time for your wedding party and your vendors, the ceremony and celebration itself, and cleanup afterwards.

* Are we the only wedding taking place that day?
* How early can we come to dress?
* Is there a designated private place we can change clothes,
leave valuables or just hang out?
* How long can the wedding last?
* Do you charge a fee if it runs long?

* Noise *

While you don't want to give the impression that you are the wildest group to ever host a wedding, you do want to know what the parameters are if the wedding lasts well into the night.

* How late can the band play?
* Have neighbors ever complained about noise?
* Have you ever had to stop a wedding early because of noise complaints?

* Outside Vendors *

You may be perfectly happy with what the venue offers, but if you plan to handle certain aspects yourself or hire any outside vendors for planning, decorating, catering or bartending, be sure you are clear on the venue's guidelines. Many have restrictions on using unlicensed vendors or non-professionals, so it's important to ask very specific questions in this area. Here are a few suggestions:

* If I use a wedding planner, how early will they have access to the venue?
* Can rental companies drop off early?
* Can we do our own setup? If so, when? Is your staff available to assist if needed?
* Can we use our own caterers or prepare the food ourselves?
* Can I or my caterers use your kitchen facilities for cooking or heating?
* Can we bring in our own liquor, wine and beer?
* Do you require a bonded or licensed bartender?
* Does everything need to be taken down the night of the wedding? (You don't want to end your glorious day trying to untangle thousands of little white lights!)

SOMETIMES THE BEST WAY TO FIT ALL YOUR GUESTS IN A SPACE IS TO
MIX THE SHAPES OF YOUR TABLES. TABLES IN ROUND, SQUARE AND
RECTANGLE SHAPES ARE FUN TO USE TOGETHER.

* Important Details *

Take the time to get into the logistical aspects of the venue. Contracts, insurance, parking, handicapped access and restrooms all fall into this category. They're not the most glamorous parts to consider, but hammering out these details can make a huge difference in ensuring your wedding day goes as smoothly as possible.

* Is there a contract to sign?
* Is any of our deposit refundable if we have to cancel? If so, how much?
* When and how are deposits returned?
* Does the venue require that we get our own liability insurance policy for the day?
* Do we have to clean or make ready any of the buildings or locations?
(Think dusty barns or overgrown meadows.)
* Can I use real candles at the venue? (This is particularly important to know about
for barns and wooden structures.)
* Is there a plan B if the weather does not cooperate?
* Is there plenty of convenient parking or will we need to hire a valet service?
* Do we need to acquire any permits from the local area?
* Is there easy access to all the event spaces and restrooms for handicapped guests?
* Are the restrooms permanent or portable, and will there be enough to comfortably
accommodate a party of our size?

* Outdoor Activities *

Ask any of the questions that might relate to your own special dreamy plans, even if they're not yet set in stone. You won't be able to foresee all of these details at the time you pick a venue, but it's still worthwhile to ask ahead and cover your bases.

* Can we have a bonfire?
* Can we play lawn games?
* Are there any other restrictions or guidelines to using the property that we have not covered?
* Is there a proper flat space for tents?

A CANOE OFFERS A PERFECT PHOTO OPPORTUNITY WHEN HAVING A LAKESIDE AFFAIR.

* Check References *

Certainly ask for the thoughts of anyone you know who hosted their wedding at a venue you are considering. Most people are only too happy to share their experiences! Read as many reviews online as possible, but beware of any that are too biased either way. Perhaps most importantly, talk to local vendors who have worked with the venue. Caterers, florists, bakers, wedding planners, rental companies and other wedding professionals often have valuable behind-the-scenes insights to offer. They can share with you the pros and cons that will help you weigh your choices before making a final decision.

Once you have settled on a venue, go all in. They are now your partners in planning the big day. Don't be afraid to hold their feet to the fire on things they promised, but be understanding if and when you have to compromise.

Most couples are extremely happy with the place they settle on and have a wonderful day. Just remember, even though no venue is perfect, your wedding will be!

"To me, it's all about finding the perfect venue. You want to find just the right kind of rustic place you fall in love with, and all of the little details will fall into place. We found a beautiful old barn for our wedding, which really speaks for itself." —LISA F., BRIDE-TO-BE

WHO: THE CROWD

From small, intimate weddings to large celebrations bustling with friends and family, getting a handle on how many guests you intend to host will have a major impact on the budget, venue choice and so many other elements of your planning. Most couples have a general idea of what size their wedding will be, but unless you are envisioning something ultra small, it's best to take a quick count of how many friends and family will be on the list. Don't forget to check in with parents and grandparents; you will want an idea of who and how many people they would like to include, as well. While the guest list will inevitably change a little over time, getting started on it early and having a ballpark number in mind will help with many future decisions.

FACING, LOWER RIGHT: A BRIDE AND HER BRIDESMAIDS HOP ABOARD A TROLLEY TO HEAD TO THE RECEPTION.

Maggie's Tip

For a complete list of venues, check out my very carefully curated list of rustic venues at RusticWeddingGuide.com. Here are a few venues around the country that I adore:

» THE HOLLY FARM, Carmel, California
» HOLLAND RANCH, San Luis Obispo, California
» MONTESINO RANCH, Wimberley, Texas
» VISTA WEST RANCH, Dripping Springs, Texas
» CROOKED WILLOW FARM, Larkspur, Colorado
» FOUR SEASONS HOTEL, Denver, Colorado
» THE PEAKS, Telluride, Colorado
» CEDARWOOD, Nashville, Tennessee
» BLACKBERRY FARMS, Walland, Texas
» THE ENCHANTED BARN, Hillsdale, Wisconsin
» WHITEFACE LODGE, Lake Placid, New York
» THE BARN AT HARDY FARM, Fryeburg, Maine

CHAPTER TWO

STYLE INSPIRATION

FINDING YOUR RUSTIC WEDDING STYLE

DESIGNING A WEDDING IS A FUN AND CREATIVE PROCESS, yet it can be challenging and overwhelming at times, too. Thanks to wedding blogs like Rustic Wedding Chic and the popularity of sites like Pinterest, there is an unending amount of wedding inspiration to take in. The best way to organize your thoughts and harness all the inspiration floating around out there is to drill down to the very core of what type of wedding day you and your partner want. Take note of landscapes, atmospheres and aesthetics that resonate with each of you and then map out the steps to get there.

Inspiration may strike out like lightning or it may be an image that you've loved for years. Whatever the source, it is the foundation on which you will build your wedding-day dreams. Although you may have thought that wanting a rustic wedding narrowed the field to a singular style, you need to be even more specific. The word "rustic" is really an umbrella term for a variety of wedding styles. A country-style wedding and an industrial-style wedding still fall into the rustic wedding category, despite their aesthetic differences. To break it down a little further, here is my guide to the six most popular rustic wedding styles to help you visualize what sort of rustic theme resonates with you the most.

* Country *

An elegant country wedding is one of the most beautiful rustic wedding styles. Envision an open field with rolling farmland and pastoral backdrops. Rooted in the simplicity of idyllic farm life, a country wedding can be as elegant or casual an affair as you see fit.

Brides are embracing the country style and making it all their own. For years, gorgeous country brides have been pairing their elegant wedding gowns with rugged cowboy boots for a fun, irreverent take on bridal footwear. In recent years, the trend has caught on across the country and within wedding parties themselves—bridesmaids are wearing boots with their dresses, too!

COUNTRY WEDDING
DECORATION IDEAS

burlap
lace
birch
vintage fabrics
mason jars
lanterns
quilts
chalkboards

Maggie's Tip

Many hardware stores and home goods emporiums sell items such as Mason jars and burlap that can be transformed into magical wedding goodies. Make sure to add these stores to your shopping list when looking for countrified wedding items.

* *Classic Rustic* *

Steeped in nostalgia, camps, lodges and barns are just a few of the classic rustic locations for a wedding. From birch bark vases to s'mores favors for guests, the classic rustic wedding is rife with opportunity to throw an unforgettable event. Like something out of a *Field & Stream* magazine from the fifties, a classic rustic wedding is the most romantic take on what we all love about the great outdoors.

RUSTIC WEDDING
VENUE IDEAS
....

camps
lodges
barns
ranches
farms
vineyards

* Industrial *

Industrial rustic weddings are one of the styles I have seen become more and more popular in recent years. For that cool industrial chic look, think about hosting your wedding at an old factory, loft space or historical building. This wedding style offers plenty of opportunity for repurposing utilitarian items and salvaged finds into wedding décor treasures.

INDUSTRIAL WEDDING COLOR PALETTE IDEAS

gold and white
black and white
mint green and silver
brown and cream
metallics

Maggie's Tip

Head over to one of my favorite sites called ThePerfectPalette.com, where you will find hours of wedding color inspiration. This site is fun because you can search by color or season to design the perfect color combo.

Backyard

Backyard nuptials make for some of the most special rustic weddings. This intimate, familiar space allows the bride and groom to create their own wedding look from top to bottom. A lavish tented reception and an al fresco picnic-style wedding are equally enchanting and can be tailored to fit most any budget. One preconceived notion about a backyard wedding is that they are always casual in nature, but backyard weddings can be as formal or as footloose as the bride and groom desire. The charm of lawn games, barbeque dinners and dancing under a canopy of string lights are just a few enticing reasons to consider the potential right in your own backyard.

EASY BACKYARD WEDDING CENTERPIECE IDEAS

lemons and limes	moss
pinecones	wine corks
rocks	pumpkins
lanterns	potted plants
apples	acorns
shells	

* Barn *

Of course, I consider barns to be a perfect wedding location, evidenced by the entire book I dedicated to the subject. As much as I loved it before, since writing *Barn Weddings* I have an even greater appreciation for the unique romance a barn wedding evokes. I truly believe there is a barn out there for every wedding.

Whether you prefer the classic red barn or an open-sided party barn, brides often struggle with the challenge of decorating such a cavernous space. Most are so vast that to decorate each and every section would be outside the realm of possibility and practicality. My favorite way to tackle this challenge is to define intimate spaces within the barn through the lighting design. It's the most efficient way to create a gorgeous, warm environment without breaking the bank.

BARN WEDDING FAVOR IDEAS

honey
jam
s'mores
maple syrup
sapling tree
flower seeds
pine sachet
herbs
stick pencils

Maggie's
Tip

A great place to look for wedding favors is on Etsy.com. From jam to honey to cookie cutters, you will find the most perfect wedding favors!

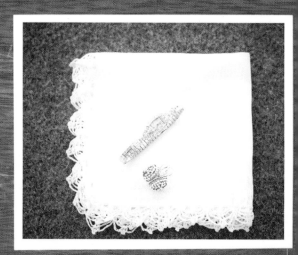

* Vintage *

The opportunity to invoke the beauty of a bygone era is just one of many reasons why brides and couples are flocking to a vintage-style wedding. Through repurposed furniture and hand-crafted details, a vintage-inspired look is always as unique as the couple who plans it.

VINTAGE WEDDING
FLOWER IDEAS

baby's-breath
peonies
roses
hydrangea
orchids
lily of the valley
hyacinth

Maggie's
Tip

Most large cities have a floral market, making it the perfect location to find floral inspiration. Floral markets are filled with floral experts so they are great places to go and connect with the best in the industry. A few famous markets include the Original Flower Market in LA, the NYC Flower Market in Manhattan and the Boston Flower Market.

CHAPTER THREE

HUNTING & GATHERING

BEFORE YOU START SHOPPING

AS YOU HEAD OUT TO THE MARKETS AND SHOPS TO FIND THAT ONE-OF-A-KIND WEDDING DAY DÉCOR, keep in mind my tips to stay on track, on budget and on style. Remember these three maxims the next time you are scouring antiques stores, flea markets or floral marts: bring cash, arrive early and stay on track.

Although most shopping destinations accept credit cards in our wonderful age of technology, flea markets in particular remain a cash-driven place. It's worthwhile to have cash on hand for your purchases so you never miss out on a great find. Along with having cash in hand, arriving early is the name of the game when it comes to finding the best vintage items to work into your wedding day décor. Many flea markets and shops refresh their inventory after hours, so you will have the highest chance of finding what you need early in the morning. This third and final piece of advice is usually the hardest to follow. When surrounded by so many fun items, sometimes you'll find yourself drawn to things that don't have much to do with the task at hand. Try to keep your focus as narrow as possible. I know—easier said than done!

{ Before }

{ After }

WHERE TO HUNT & GATHER FOR
YOUR WEDDING DAY DÉCOR

* Flea Markets *

One of my favorite spots to find interesting wedding day décor is at the flea market. Not only do flea markets provide great vintage items, but many times you can find vendors selling items in bulk, which can save you time and money.

VASES AND MASON JARS: Creating the perfect wedding centerpiece goes way beyond the type of flowers you select. Clustering together unique vases in interesting colors, shapes and vintage styles is a great way to create a dynamic display. Vases for this type of display can be found at almost any flea market. Here I transformed average blue bottles by adding crisp white flowers and pairing them with a larger collection of similar-colored vases.

THE MOMENT I SAW THESE LITTLE BLUE VASES I KNEW THAT THEY COULD BE PERFECT AS PART OF A LARGER CENTERPIECE IDEA. I MIXED AND MATCHED A VARIETY OF VASE SHAPES ALL IN THE SAME COLOR TO MAKE THE PERFECT RUSTIC WEDDING CENTERPIECE.

VINTAGE BOOKS: There is something ridiculously romantic about vintage books. Add them into your wedding day repertoire to bring some old-school romance to your day. These classic items work beautifully as centerpieces and ring pillows and can even be repurposed into one-of-a-kind table numbers. One of my favorite ways to use books at a wedding is to simply stack them up and use them as the base of a centerpiece.

Maggie's Tip

Frames do not have to cost a bundle to look great. Even frames from the dollar store can be "wedding day ready" by adding a coat of shimmering spray paint, a touch of gold or silver sequins or just wrapped in twine. Here are a few nation-wide stores that offer good-looking inexpensive frames:

» IKEA
» MICHAEL'S CRAFT STORE
» HOMEGOODS

» HOBBY LOBBY
» WORLD MARKET
» AC MOORE

FRAMES: With or without glass, frames are wonderful for hanging place cards, creating table numbers or for fun photo booth props.

I CAN THINK OF COUNTLESS WAYS TO USE FRAMES AT A WEDDING. THESE PASTEL FINDS FROM A FLEA MARKET ARE PERFECT FOR A SPRING WEDDING THEME.

FABRIC: There is no end to the ways you can include vintage-style fabric in your wedding. Large rolls of fabric can be transformed into everything from table runners and tablecloths to napkins, chair swags, photo booth and ceremony backdrops, or placed over bales of hay for easy seating. Find a great pattern and start decorating!

DISPLAY PIECES: Every wedding has items that need to be displayed for guests to see, take or eat. I found this simple red stepstool at a flea market, and I was able to repurpose it into the perfect rustic wedding cupcake tower.

Need a sign for your guest book table? Inject some personality with a little treasure like this one I found from an iron dealer at a North Carolina flea market (see page 58).

FABRIC, FABRIC AND MORE FABRIC! THIS WAS THE FIRST BOOTH I SAW (AND FELL IN LOVE WITH) WHEN SHOPPING AT A NORTH CAROLINA FLEA MARKET. ARRANGED BY COLOR, THIS BOOTH WAS BOTH FUN AND EASY TO SHOP.

SMALL CAST IRON LITTLE ANIMALS ARE FUN TREASURES THAT CAN BE
PLACED JUST ABOUT ANYWHERE IN YOUR DECORATING.

TRINKETS AND TREASURES: If you are thinking of adding a unique cake topper, check the flea market for trinkets that can be repurposed into something truly unique. On a recent shopping trip I found loads of sweet pairs and mismatched items that could easily be used as cake toppers. One of my favorite finds is a set of metal animals that look both vintage and oh-so-cute sitting on top of a simple wedding cake.

Most people don't think "wedding" when they see an entire flea market booth of vintage fishing rods, but, between the colors and the masculine rustic style, I knew I could find a way to use them. I envisioned them as an unexpected way to hang the escort cards, and, lo and behold, after a little work they looked so perfectly rustic.

Even something as unusual as vintage metal stamp holders can be used in your wedding day décor. I stopped in my tracks when I found a pair sitting out on a table at a flea market. I knew I could make them into the perfect vase for small spray roses.

"I'm constantly reminding myself that less is more. I'll have a design or setup that I think is perfect, but when I take a step back and really look at it, there is almost always something that can be removed. I remove that element and only then is it perfect!"
—KRISTIN AUSTIN, PAIGE SIMPLE STUDIO

{ *Before* }

Perusing a flea market down in North Carolina, I found an old tackle box in a stunning green color. When I spotted it, I knew there was no way I could pass it up. For just $8, I scored a uniquely beautiful way to display flowers.

{ *After* }

{ Before }

Don't walk away from a flea market without looking for items that can be used as creative place-card materials. I found simple, classic horseshoes to make into country-chic escort cards and they double as favors.

HORSESHOES CAN OFTEN BE FOUND IN BLACK AND SILVER, BUT DON'T FORGET THAT A SIMPLE CAN OF SPRAY PAINT CAN TRANSFORM THIS COUNTRY ITEM INTO SOMETHING SPECIAL.

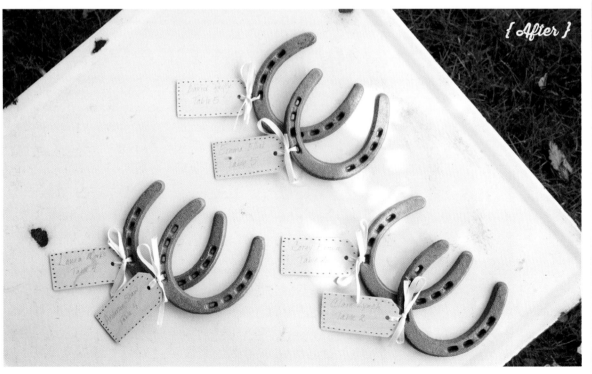

{ After }

UNIQUE GUEST BOOK: Unusual items such as a vintage surfboard or a classic globe can be transformed into the perfect guest book. One thing to keep in mind when selecting a guest book is to take into account the number of people who will sign the item. If you're hosting a large wedding, then two guest books may be needed.

"Be original! Think of a fun, unique guest book. Try a homemade quilt or get a fun prop— guitar, oars or Adirondack chairs—and have your guests sign away!"
—ASHLEE FROM ASHLEE VIRGINIA EVENTS

MONOGRAM MATERIAL: Couples love to add their new monogram to their wedding décor in a variety of ways. Monograms look fabulous on top of the cake, hanging from the sweetheart table or as a backdrop at the ceremony location. Gorgeous monogram material awaits you at the flea market.

I found oversized letters in different colors and materials that, when combined, bring a vintage vibe to an otherwise traditional monogram. Even something as simple as two pillows with great graphics can be used as a type of monogram.

MISMATCHED SEATING AND FURNITURE: Many couples want to add just a few signature vintage and rustic design elements to their design. A simple way to achieve this look is to have one or two large-scale items mixed into your wedding day décor. I love it when a dresser is reimagined as a cake table or as a place to display key design elements.

LARGE FURNITURE MIGHT BE SOMETHING
YOU WANT TO INVEST IN FOR YOUR
WEDDING DAY DECORATING. PIECES
SUCH AS CHAIRS, TABLES AND DRESSERS
CAN LATER BE USED IN YOUR HOME.

Maggie's Tip

Mixing and matching furniture is fun, but it is also an art form. After all, you want it to look more like a great vintage store and not a flea market. Many event planners and vintage rental companies can help you figure out the best way to mix and match your vintage items. Here are a few furniture items that can look great repurposed at a wedding:

» DRESSERS
» BENCHES
» DINING CHAIRS
» COUCHES AND LOUNGE AREA
  SETTINGS

Insider's Tips for Flea Market Success

GET THERE EARLY: Many flea markets and antiques shows open their doors early. Grab a cup of coffee and reserve your space in line so when the doors open, you get the best selection. Oftentimes an "early bird" entrance pass is available, but they can cost anywhere up to $20, depending on the market. You don't have to buy your way into every market, but, as the saying goes, the early bird gets the worm.

HAVE CASH: Even with so much wonderful technology and recent tools made for small vendors such as the Square credit card reader, cash is still king at the flea market. Ninety-nine percent of markets run on a cash-only policy, so hit the ATM before you start shopping. Since it's common knowledge that the shoppers have cash on them at these markets, tuck your cash securely away and only pull it out when you need it to pay for something to avoid becoming a target for pickpockets.

KEEP SMALL BILLS NEARBY: Keep small bills such as ones and fives handy for fast buys, snacks and water breaks so you won't have to pull out your big bills as often.

WEAR COMFY CLOTHES AND PACK FOR INCLEMENT WEATHER: Blisters, wet feet and being over or underdressed are all part of earning your flea market stripes, but you can avoid such suffering while snapping up great deals by being prepared. Check the weather forecast and take an umbrella (useful for both rain and sun). Bonus insider's tip: Pack an extra pair of socks in your purse in case your feet get wet. Even if there isn't a rain cloud in sight, you never know when they are going to come in handy. I once whipped out my extra socks and used them as gloves to go through a box of goodies that were a little less than clean.

ALWAYS ASK FOR MORE: Vendors don't want to overcrowd their booths for aesthetic reasons, so they might only display a small portion of their inventory. If a set of shutters catches your eye but you would need an addi-tional set to make the perfect place-card display, always ask if they have more. Vendors will often have addition-al items in their truck.

MAKE A LIST: Heading to the markets is no different than shopping at the grocery store—if you don't have a target list of items, you are in danger of ending up with more than you really want or need. Make a list of the items you are looking for and how many you would ideally need. If shopping with friends, give a copy to every-one—the more eyes on the prize, the better.

LISTEN AND CHAT: If you're waiting in line for the restroom or for a bottle of water, use this downtime to chat with your fellow shoppers. They can be your best source of information for what's out there in the field. You might just receive a tip about a vendor in a distant corner of the market who has an entire outlet of old-fashioned school supplies. In wedding lingo, this translates to tons of different-sized chalkboards just waiting to be snatched up and put to use in a rustic design scheme. Score!

BRING IMAGES: If you are hunting for wedding items, then you are probably becoming fully immersed in the bridal world. But don't assume that all vendors will know what you are talking about when using wedding terminology. Don't be shy! Pull some images from maga-zines and wedding books to give vendors a visual refer-ence point. It can help jog their memories for inventory they have on display or in their trucks.

GET IN TOUCH: Many vendors have brick-and-mortar shops, websites or storage facilities with additional mer-chandise. Print and bring cards with your name, phone number and email. If a vendor has something you're looking for but not at this particular show, having a card with your contact information on hand is an easy way to keep the dialogue going and ultimately get your hands on that special piece.

Maggie's Tip:
Flea Markets I Love
and Have Shopped
Myself

» BROOKLYN FLEA, Brooklyn, New York
» BRIMFIELD, Brimfield, Massachusetts
» THE ELEPHANT'S TRUNK, New Milford,
  Connecticut
» RALEIGH FLEA MARKET, Raleigh,
  North Carolina
» ROSE BOWL FLEA MARKET, Pasadena California

Maggie's Tip

Here are a few of my favorite wedding stationery designers:

» MINTED
» WEDDING PAPER DIVAS
» THE BLUE ENVELOPE
» LOVE VS. DESIGN
» AUGUST PARK CREATIVE
» STEEL PETAL PRESS

Wedding Paper & Stationery Pieces to Consider Ordering

» SAVE THE DATES
» REHEARSAL DINNER INVITATIONS
» INVITATION SUITES
» WEDDING LOCATION MAPS
» WEDDING PROGRAMS
» MENU CARDS
» PLACE CARDS OR ESCORT CARDS
» TABLE NUMBERS
» THANK YOU CARDS
» PERSONALIZED STATIONERY WITH NEW MONOGRAM

* Unique & Specialty Shops *

Assembling all the components of your wedding décor means finding items from a variety of sources. Since there really is no one-stop shop, part of the fun is looking at shops that have either new or used items or a combination of the two. You can find beautiful, useful wedding items at local boutiques, antiques shops, even national chain stores like Ikea and Target. You just have to know what to look for.

One of the largest investments in a wedding is the save the dates, invitations and paper products. There are a wide variety of online sources where you can find designs and order your custom wedding paper items, but don't forget that there are still old-fashioned stationery stores that specialize in wedding stationery that might be able to help you as well. Sitting down with a stationery expert might help you navigate through the vast world of terms and decisions and in the end help ensure that your wedding invitation is perfect.

VINTAGE ITEMS CAN BE ENTICING TO BUY BUT MAKE SURE YOU GIVE CUPS, PLATES AND OTHER ITEMS THE ONCEOVER BEFORE BUYING TO MAKE SURE THERE ARE NO CRACKS OR CHIPS.

GLASS CONTAINERS IN A VARIETY OF SIZES ARE AN EASY WAY TO DISPLAY EVERYTHING FROM CANDY TO TISSUES. CHECK OUT STORES LIKE IKEA THAT ALWAYS HAVE AN IMPRESSIVE SELECTION OF GLASS ITEMS.

* Farmers Markets *

You can find more than just fruits and veggies at the farmers market. These seasonal markets are the perfect place to find vendors with handcrafted pieces such as wooden table numbers and rustic wedding signs along with goodies like edible favors to send home with guests. Many vendors at farmers markets will have items like jam, honey or even trail mix, which can be transformed into great down-home wedding favors. Here I used simple spice jars from Ikea and filled them with trail mix for a budget-friendly favor and perennial crowd pleaser (see lower photo, facing page).

Dreaming of the perfect rustic wedding dessert table? Talk to the bakers at your local farmers market. I guarantee one of them will be able to make your wedding cake or wedding pie dreams a reality.

* Hardware Stores *

The hardware store is probably not the first place that comes to mind when searching for wedding items, but it happens to be one of my favorite spots to look for great ideas and inspiration along with useful, practical items.

BUCKETS AND BINS: Buckets and bins of all sizes will always come in handy at a wedding. Use them to set up a colorful candy bar for guests, display your wedding programs or fill a few with flip-flops at the reception to save guests' dancing feet. Hardware stores are a great place to find these containers in a large assortment of sizes, shapes and finishes, whether you want a galvanized bucket or a more refined container.

PAINT SECTION: Head to the paint section of your local hardware store to find color upon gorgeous color and endless inspiration. When selecting a wedding color palette, seeing the colors together in a fan deck can be a great place to start to narrow down your options or expand your horizons. Mixing and matching paint swatches will help you visualize how the color families work together and play off one another. There are so many choices, but rest assured that there is a perfect palette for every wedding.

LUMBER: Sometimes the best wedding décor items are those that can be made with just a few simple items: wood, nails and paint. Want to make a unique wedding menu board? Pick up a few large, square pieces of wood, paint them white, and write out your wedding day menu.

It can be a challenge for couples to find the perfect guest book that is both practical and unique, but one trip to your local hardware store can solve this conundrum. Purchase a piece of wood and have it cut right there in the store into a unique shape that suits your wishes. One coat of white paint later, you have a perfect rustic wedding guest book and a great-looking keepsake to hang in your home.

* Garden Centers *

Flowers are often the main design element at a wedding, so spend some time getting to know the different varieties available for your wedding day at a local garden center or nursery. Inspiration for your wedding's floral design can be built around a single flower, flower family or even a flower color. Talk with a floral professional to see what will be in season around your wedding date and what works well together. They may also have great ideas about incorporating succulents, moss and other greenery into your design.

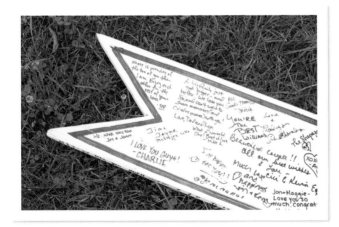

SIMPLE COUNTRY WEDDINGS CALL FOR SIMPLE COUNTRY DECORATIONS, WHICH ARE SEEN
HERE WITH GINGHAM ROUND BOXES, AN ARROW GUEST BOOK AND A PITCHER VASE.

5 Unique Ways to Display Flowers

» WOOD BOXES

» BIRCH VASES

» RECYCLED BOTTLES

» BUCKETS AND BINS

» ON BRANCHES

FLOWERS ARE USUALLY ONE OF THE MAIN DECORATIONS AT A WEDDING, SO MAKE SURE YOU TAKE THE TIME TO FIND THE PERFECT CONTAINER FOR YOUR FLOWERS. IF YOU ARE THINKING OF TAKING ON THE FLOWERS AS A DIY PROJECT, MAKE SURE YOU CONSULT A LOCAL FLORIST WHO CAN HELP YOU SELECT THE RIGHT CONTAINER FOR EACH FLOWER.

* Rental Services *

Gathering all of the decorations, linens and tableware for a rustic wedding is not an easy task. In fact, I have seen many rental companies specializing in vintage and rustic décor spring up recently to address this bridal market need. Renting some items is a great alternative to trying to find every single must-have on your list. Rentals combined with a few key wedding items that you source or make yourself ensures that your style and personality will be stamped on the day without over-extending yourself.

I recently spent the day with Heidi Hill-Haddard, the owner of the unique shop HiHo Home Market in Gardiner, New York. Among all the amazing new and antique items she stocks, Heidi also specializes in vintage wedding rentals. While at her store, Heidi gave me her insights on what brides should buy and what they are better off renting for a rustic chic wedding.

Wedding Décor Shopping Dos & Don'ts

DO have a list of items that you know you want at your wedding, and always bring a visual with you when shopping.

DO stick to a budget. It's easy to spend more than you should, but breaking your budget down into these three sections for the wedding décor will help you stay on target: ceremony, cocktail hour, and reception.

DON'T buy the first thing you see. When shopping a farmers market or flea market, you might have the impulse to buy that first set of beautiful vintage tablecloths you find. Take your time and avoid buyer's remorse by doing a lap around the market before making any big decisions.

DO snap a quick pic of your purchases to keep a running visual list of what you bought and how many you have. This will help you avoid overbuying, too.

DON'T stray from your original design theme. If you want a modern rustic look, avoid vintage-style items. Resist the urge to buy every cute thing (there will be a lot!) and stay true to your design theme. Your wedding day décor will be more cohesive and better off because of it.

DON'T start buying without a firm idea of your guest list for the wedding. From the ballpark number of people you expect, determine how many tables you'll be dressing, an important figure when budgeting for and buying reception pieces.

WINDOW FRAMES HAVE BECOME A HOT ITEM TO USE IN WEDDING DECORATING. RECENTLY I HAVE SEEN COUPLES USE THE GLASS IN THE FRAME TO SHOWCASE THE MENU FOR THE RECEPTION, HIGHLIGHT WHO THE WEDDING PARTY MEMBERS ARE OR JUST TO WRITE LOVE NOTES.

I HAD A FIELD DAY WHEN POKING AROUND HIHO HOME MARKET IN GARDINER, NEW YORK, AND
AMONG THE TREASURES WHERE MISMATCHED TEACUPS AND SILVER FORKS.

Maggie's Tip

Rental companies do not have an endless supply of goods, so make sure you talk with your rental company early in the planning process. Many companies only have one of a particular item, so if you want something specific, make sure you have a meeting with your rental company and ask for what you will want or need.

HEIDI'S RENT VS. BUY LIST

RENT

Vintage and new dessert and cake table items have the biggest wow factor.

» *Plates:* Pedestal cake plates help make dessert tables look lovely. Plates in assorted patterns and a variety of sizes are charming additions to tablescapes.

» *Glassware:* New stemware for toasting and new coffee cups and mugs are perfect (vintage cups and saucers look wonderful but are challenging when it comes to size and breakage).

» *Cutlery:* Vintage dessert forks are so special and remind your guests just how important that cake is.

» *Tablecloths and napkins:* Linens and worrying about laundry can be a daunting part of this category.

BUY

Consider purchasing a signature piece or two that you will have forever, something in your style that can fit into your everyday life and of a high enough quality to be handed down. A wedding has the ability to take an ordinary object and turn it into a family heirloom. I recommend it be a piece that will be photographed throughout the day such as vintage sweetheart chairs, a small table for the cake, gifts, place cards or a sideboard or buffet serving piece.

Vintage mirrors are magical and make great purchases, too; you and your bridesmaids will use them all day.

Purchase the vessels for your flowers. Guests often grab these arrangements on the way out, and you don't want to have to settle up with the rental company.

Buy some additional lighting, it adds romance and makes the space your own.

Maggie's Tip

Talk with an event planner who will be able to help make your day run effortlessly. Here are a few event planners who I feel are some of the best in the rustic wedding business:

» RAMBLING HOUSE EVENT & FOOD DESIGN, Nashua, New Hampshire
» GOLD LEAF EVENT DESIGN & PRODUCTIONS, Aspen, Colorado
» BALBOA WEDDINGS & EVENTS, Riverside, California
» FORGET ME NOT EVENTS, Kingston, New York

REPURPOSING FURNITURE INTO A WEDDING DECORATION IS ONE OF MY MOST FAVORITE IDEAS AND USUALLY IS AN UNEXPECTED SIGHT FOR GUESTS.

CHAPTER FOUR

DIY PROJECTS

DECORATIONS FOR
THE BIG DAY

I ALWAYS CHUCKLE AT THE TERM "DO IT YOUR-SELF" (DIY for short) since almost any wedding project requires a team. Considering how popular DIY projects have become on the wedding scene, I think it is important for crafters to remember it "takes a village" of your nearest and dearest to plan and decorate for the big day. Semantics aside, I think what draws rustic brides to the DIY style is the opportunity to inject an extra measure of personality and creativity into their wedding day projects. This handbook would not be complete without a few DIY rustic wedding ideas to get you started down the crafting road. It's not nearly as easy or as fun to do these alone, so I teamed up with one of my favorite event planning and design teams for an all-out crafting weekend in a charming New Hampshire barn. Erin, Jillian and Kerry are the ladies behind Rambling House Events & Design, and together we came up with a few DIY concepts that will make your rustic wedding truly unique.

THRIFTED TEACUP CANDLES

Add a little bit of vintage whimsy to your wedding with these homemade teacup candles. These candles will look charming on your wedding dinner tables, as romantic lighting surrounding your escort cards or just to add some drama around your wedding cake.

Tools & Materials

» Beeswax pellets

» Matching or assorted teacups

» Cookie sheet

» New wicking

» Optional: wick sustainers, wooden skewers

* Instructions *

1. Preheat your oven to 250 degrees Fahrenheit, and have a cookie sheet on standby.

2. Cut your wick to be 1 inch above the length of the teacup, to allow for trimming at the end.

Holding the wick above the teacup, with the other end touching the bottom, fill the teacup with beeswax pellets. Be sure to hold the wick straight at the middle as you fill, to ensure that it sits evenly as the wax sets. Do not hesitate to fill the teacup to the top—the pellets will melt down, leaving substantial empty space. If you find it difficult to hold the wick yourself, use sustainers to anchor the wick to the bottom of the teacup.

By tying the top of the wick to a wooden skewer, and laying the skewer along the top of the teacup, you can keep the wick straight in the middle, and out of the way of the melting wax. Be careful, because if the wick falls into the wax, you no longer have a candle!

3. Set up your teacups on a cookie sheet and place them in your preheated oven. Allow the wax to melt completely. Smaller teacups will take approximately a half hour, while large teacups will melt in approximately an hour.

4. When the wax is completely melted, turn off the oven. Leave the teacups in the oven until they have completely set—removing them will cause cracking and splitting in the wax.

5. Cut the wick to your desired length.

6. To scent the candles, add one or two drops of your favorite essential oil. Beeswax does have its own clean, natural scent, but soy candles are easy and fun to add fragrance to, as well.

Maggie's Tip

A few great places to find teacups for this project:

» GOODWILL
» THRIFT STORES
» YOUR MOTHER'S ATTIC
» RESTAURANT SUPPLY STORES
» FLEA MARKETS
» GOING-OUT-OF-BUSINESS SALES

DOILY TABLE RUNNER

A doily table runner adds a touch of grace and femininity to a rustic event, without adding too much frill. If you don't want to take on creating a table runner for each table, you don't have to worry. Think about creating a doily table runner for just key tables such as escort card table, the guest book table, or where you display favors.

* Tools & Materials *

» Assorted crocheted doilies
» Needle
» Cream or white thread
» Measuring tape

* Instructions *

1. Check out a local thrift or antiques shop for doilies. Buy an assortment of sizes and designs, depending on how cohesive or eclectic you'd like your table runner to look. For a shabby-chic look, mix up the shapes and sizes—even the fabric shades can differ.

2. Measure the length of your table. Be sure to add about 5 to 6 inches on each end if you want your table runner to hang over the edges.

3. Before attaching the doilies, align them on the table in a desired pattern.

4. Try out a few different patterns before making your decision. We liked a more symmetrical look, with matching patterns on each side of the center of our runner. For a more eclectic look, mix and match to your heart's content.

5. Once you have your desired pattern and length, thread your needle. Starting at one end, begin attaching the doilies. Tie the ends together loosely, so as to not bunch the doilies. Attempt to keep all of the ties on the bottom of the doilies, to hide the signs of threading.

6. When all of the doilies are attached, try out your new runner! Top it with a personalized centerpiece on the day of the event.

RUSTIC FLORAL PHOTO BOOTH BACKDROP

A hanging floral backdrop adds the perfect pop of color to a wedding photo booth—it's the rustic take on the technology corner of your wedding.

Tools & Materials

- » A long dowel or decorative branch (a birch branch works perfectly)
- » Fishing wire
- » Needles (one per crafter)
- » Flowers with a thick stem/receptacle (we used Gerbera Daisies)

* Instructions *

1. Decide how tall and long you want your backdrop to be—choose the dowel or branch, and cut your fishing wire accordingly.

2. Tie each piece of fishing wire to the branch, so that the wire is hanging down in tendrils. You can tie on as many or as few as you like.

Cut the stems off the flowers. If you are using a range of colors, sort the flowers into desired patterns.

3. Attach a needle to the end of each piece of fishing wire.

4. Using the needle, thread one flower up toward the branch. You should thread through the thickest part of the flower receptacle, so the flowers face forward. Once it is threaded all the way through, loop the fishing wire around and knot it. If you don't knot the flowers, they will slide. The needle and fishing wire should hang down from the flower. Repeat this step all the way up the piece of fishing wire, spacing each flower to your liking.

5. Repeat step four on each string of fishing wire.

6. Find a spot between two trees or use a barn beam to hang your new backdrop. If you like, add a box of photo booth props, such as antique picture frames, silly masks or a homemade chalkboard for guests to write messages. Lights, camera, action!

WOODLAND CHALKBOARD MENU

A slice of wood, coated with chalkboard paint, is the perfect rustic wedding canvas! Use it to welcome your guests to the venue, as table numbers, or to display your drink menu. One trip to the hardware store and you are ready to craft this chalkboard menu.

This project can be done with store-bought chalkboard paint; however, we are using grout and latex paint so that the chalkboard can be in any color you desire. This is a great way to add a fresh take on the traditional black and green chalkboard look.

* Tools & Materials *

» 2 tablespoons unsanded grout
» 1 cup latex paint
» Disposable mixing bowl, cup, or can
» Disposable spoon
» Paintbrush
» Slab of wood
» Chalk

* Instructions *

1. Decide what surface you are going to paint. For this tutorial, we painted a slab of wood. Before beginning to paint, we sanded the slab to ensure that the paint would stick and go on smoothly and evenly.

2. Pour 1 cup of paint into your mixing bowl.

3. Measure out 2 tablespoons of unsanded grout and add to the measured paint.

4. Combine the grout and the paint. You should not be able to see any of the grout's original color when you are finished mixing.

5. Use a paintbrush to apply the paint to your surface. The paint will be much thicker than other paints you have worked with—this is normal. Apply the paint evenly and try to avoid obvious brushstrokes.

6. Allow the paint to dry completely. We let ours dry overnight, but we recommend keeping it in a dry, temperature-controlled location. Drastic changes in temperature or humidity will cause the wood to expand and then contract, creating cracks.

7. Once dry, take a piece of chalk and cover the entire chalkboard surface. This conditions the paint.

8. Erase the chalk and create your menu!

DECORATIVE PAPERED BOTTLES

A cluster of decorated bottles filled with colorful flowers makes a cute country table centerpiece! By recycling bottles you used leading up to your wedding you will not only save a few dollars on vases, but you can also offer them to your guests as they leave the reception.

* Tools & Materials *

» Scrapbooking paper

» Washi tape

» Burlap or jute paper

» Twine

» Ruler

» Scissors

» Hot glue gun

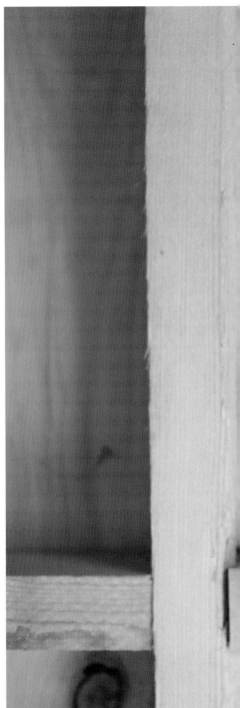

* Instructions *

1. Gather glass bottles of various shapes, sizes, and heights. We looked for bottles that did not have any branding in the actual glass, only on the label.

2. Rinse out bottles to remove any sticky residue.

3. Remove all labels from the bottles. We used a goo-removing cleaner to remove any label glue residue from the glass and then soaked the bottles in warm, soapy water. If the glue is not too stubborn, simply filling the bottles with hot water may work, as it will melt the glue from the inside. Allow the bottles to dry completely before moving to the next step.

4. For washi tape and paper vases:

Measure how tall you want the paper band to be; this can vary between bottles. (Tip: we have found that wrapping the paper around any part of the bottle's uneven curves does not work out well; we suggest only wrapping the paper around an even portion of the bottle.)

Cut the paper according to your measurements. Then wrap the paper around the bottle. Trim as necessary so that there is only a small amount of overlap from the edges of the paper.

Select which washi tape you would like to use. You can apply the washi tape to either the bottom or top of the paper—or both! Measure out your piece(s) of washi tape so they are the same length as the paper.

Wrap the paper around the bottle and adhere it with the tape, smoothing out wrinkles and bubbles in the tape as needed. The great thing about washi tape is the ease in which it can be removed, in case of mistakes.

If taping only the top or the bottom of the band, use a line of hot glue along the seam of the paper to ensure that it remains adhered to the bottle.

5. For burlap, lace and ribbon bottles:

Measure how high you would like the band of burlap around the bottle to be. Cut burlap accordingly.

Just as with the paper, loop the burlap around the bottle, and cut any excess length so that there is only a small overlap at the seam.

Use a glue gun to attach the burlap together at the seam.

Choose whether you would like to use ribbon, lace, twine, or some combination thereof to adorn the burlap. Measure the pieces and use a glue gun to attach them to the burlap.

6. Allow the glued bottles to dry thoroughly before filling with flowers or candlesticks.

RUSTIC FEATHER BOUTONNIERE

With only a few select materials, you can make a perfect rustic-style boutonniere for the groom and groomsmen. What I love about this project is the fact that you can add little details that really reflect the style you are going for.

* Tools & Materials *

» ¹/₂ inch ribbon

» ³/₄ inch ribbon

» Felt

» Feathers (found at most craft stores or online)

» Dried or live moss (found at most craft stores or online)

» Hot glue gun

» Scissors

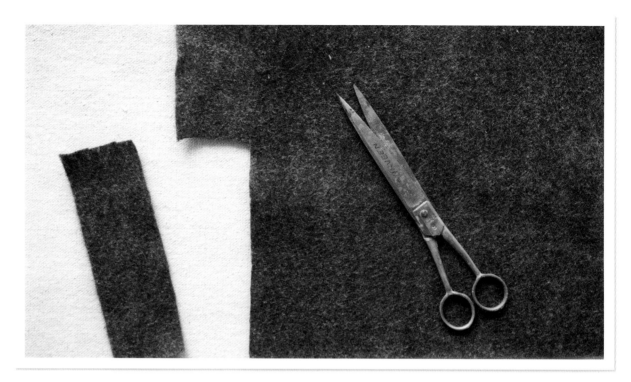

* Instructions *

1. Cut a strip of felt that is $1^{1}/_{2}$ inches wide x 4 inches long.

2. Cut a length of thin ribbon to just longer than the felt.

3. Fold felt and ribbon in half, glue ribbon to felt on either side at base and add a drop of glue to the inside of the base of the felt to hold the fold in place.

4. Using small drops of hot glue, glue the feather and moss in layers at the base of the folded felt.

5. Measure a strip of thick ribbon by wrapping it twice around the base tightly. Cut ends at opposite angles. Trim any excess ribbon, feather or moss from the base.

6. Fold in the bottom corners of the felt and secure one end of the ribbon with glue. Wrap the ribbon twice around the base, securing with glue under the end of the ribbon.

GARLAND CEREMONY BACKDROP

One creative way to save a little in your budget is to cut out a surplus of flowers for your ceremony location. A budget friendly way to still have a beautiful ceremony backdrop is to create a garland that can be hung to mimic the look of flowers without the extra cost. This garland comes in handy at the reception since it can be extra decoration.

* Tools & Materials *

- » Standard raw canvas drop cloth
- » Heavy-duty scissors
- » Masking tape
- » Pencil, regular or charcoal
- » Tracing paper
- » Needle and thread

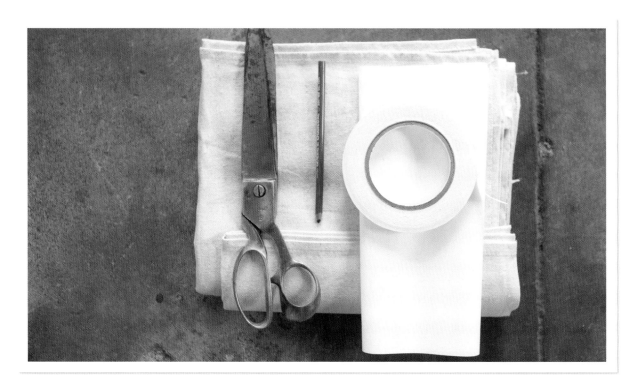

* Instructions *

1. Hand draw or trace a leafy stem design onto tracing paper, and cut out. This will be used as a stencil. The closer the leaves are to one another the fuller the garland will feel.

2. Fold a drop cloth into quarters lengthwise, and tape the stencil in place on the top layer.

3. Using the stencil, trace lightly onto the top layer of the canvas.

Maggie's Tip

Other places to hang this type of garland:

» BEHIND THE HEAD TABLE
» ABOVE THE CAKE TABLE
» THE ENTRANCE TO YOUR RECEPTION LOCATION
» AS A PHOTO BOOTH BACKDROP
» CEREMONY BACKDROP

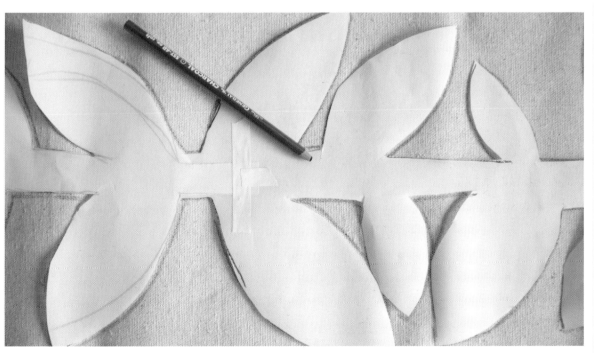

4. Cut all four layers of the canvas along the trace line and discard scraps.

5. At the end of the stencil, round off the stem to a leafy end point.

6. Pull apart the four segments. If you want to connect them to create a long garland, sew the ends together using a needle and thread until the garland is at a desired length.

7. Hang the garland in a desired place.

S'MORE STICKS

One of the most popular rustic wedding ideas is to allow guests to make some s'mores as part of the festivities. In order to allow your guests to make their own sweet treat, it's only fitting to give them the proper tools. These easy-to-make s'more sticks are both fun and functional.

* Tools & Materials *

- » Masking tape
- » Acrylic (or other non-flammable) paint
- » Sticks
- » Pencil sharpener
- » Glue gun

- » Paintbrush
- » Scissors
- » Cotton rope
- » Sandpaper

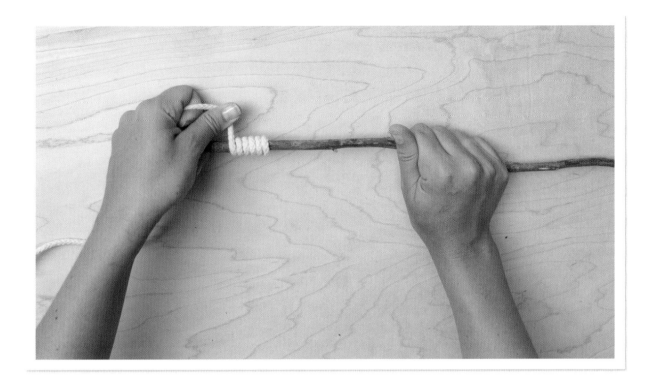

* Instructions *

1. Sharpen the ends of the sticks using a sharp knife or pencil sharpener. If splintery, use sandpaper to sand until smooth.

2. Measure cotton rope by wrapping the handle of a stick.

3. Using hot glue, secure one end of the rope to the stick and wrap the handle tightly.

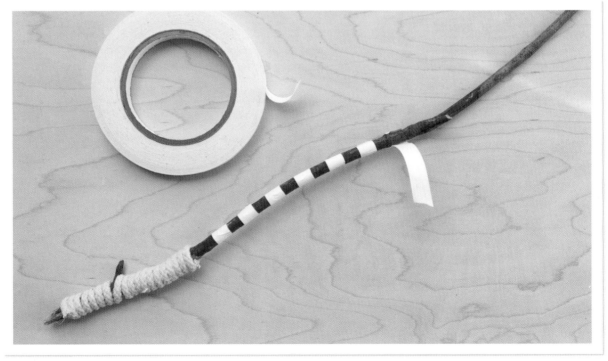

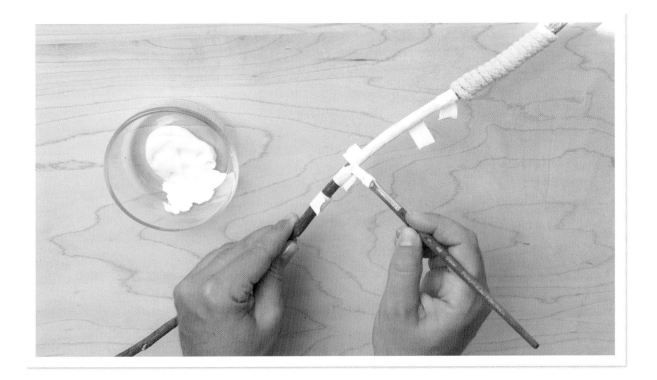

4. Then glue the other end of the rope in place at the end of the handle.

5. Using masking tape, create a stencil for the stripes you want to paint onto the sticks. Make sure the tape is tightly sealed to the stick so that the lines will be crisp.

6. Using a paintbrush, paint the exposed wood between the stencils with an even coat of paint. You may need two coats of paint.

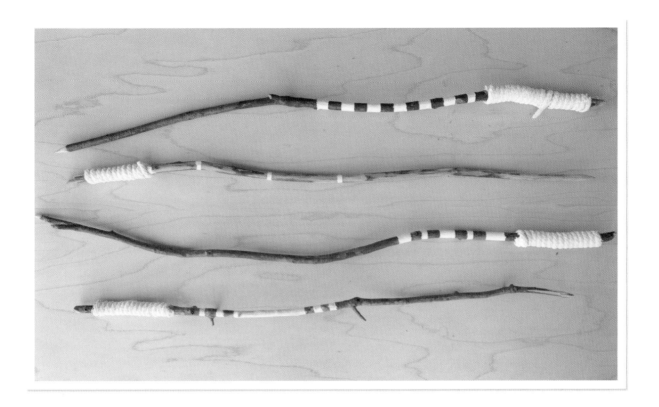

7. Then using a foam brush, paint the cotton rope with a layer of paint. Set aside to dry. When dry, carefully peel off the tape stencils and you are finished.

Maggie's Tip

A great way to ensure your guests enjoy a s'more station at your wedding is to have mini kits of all the necessary supplies: graham crackers, chocolate and marshmallows ready to go so your guests can just take and make.

STYLING A RUSTIC-CHIC SWEETHEART TABLE

A sweetheart table is a nice way to steal some time away from the busyness of picture taking, toasting, and dancing—it's a little oasis just for the newlyweds. Here are a few ways to spiff it up and make it your own.

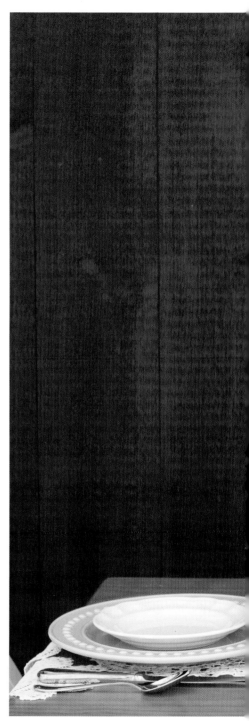

* Instructions *

1. Color palette and theme: For our table setting, we chose an upscale country color palette of warm wood, crisp white, and duck's egg blue. We made sure to keep the entire table feeling rustic yet elegant.

2. Table covering: A sweetheart table should retain simplicity, so as to not take away from the beautiful bride and groom. We chose to leave the wooden table uncovered, dressing it up with a handmade antique doily table runner. In doing this, we combined a woodsy, rustic feel with simple, graceful touches, while including both masculine and feminine elements in the décor.

3. Centerpiece: Again, we tried to select items that were polished but that still had an eclectic, handmade feel. We chose to use a few DIY paper and tape vases paired with some simple flowers. (Styling tip: When arranging, go with odd numbers! Feature one, three, or five vases instead of even-numbered groups.)

4. Silverware, flatware and glassware: In order to achieve our desired rustic look without getting kitschy, we went with a classic table setting: simple, clear glasses, white dinner plates and silver flatware. We added a pop of color with a duck's egg blue plate under each dinner plate to pull together the colors in the setting.

5. Levels and layering: Consider your table from all angles—what will it look like while sitting, standing close and standing far away, from a bird's-eye view, from the front, and from the back? Vintage books, cut pieces of wood and wine crates are great for adding height and dynamism to your tablescape. A set of three vases looks far more interesting if you stagger them up a stack of beautifully bound books! Play around with placing different elements of the table at different levels and, as we did with the blue and white dishes, layer different colors and textures to create a robust, well-executed design.

DIY Projects You Can Find on RusticWeddingChic.com

» PINE CONE FIRE STARTER FAVORS
» PAINTED VASES
» WEDDING POM POMS
» MR. & MRS. BURLAP BANNER
» BRIDESMAID CARDS
» AND MORE

CHAPTER FIVE

WEDDING DAY READY

BY NOW YOU HAVE COMPILED THE ULTIMATE COLLECTION OF WONDERFUL, WHIMSICAL, CHARMING ITEMS and a few DIY projects of your own to infuse your wedding day with fun and personality. You have checked and double checked your list and started the countdown to the big day. But how can you be sure everything is wedding day ready?

Let's start with the venue. Many rustic venues, though lovely and charming, don't always come fully outfitted for your wedding day. Even with a full-service venue, you will want to go back over major points so that there are no misunderstandings or surprises. Confirm that all vendors are on the same page in regard to the date, time and expectations. Review the agreed-upon state of the venue that you expect to find upon your arrival. Has the barn been thoroughly cleaned? Has the lawn been mowed and maintained as desired? Review the number of tables, chairs, linens or anything else that the venue will be providing or that is venue-owned.

Once you have things at the venue under control, you can start to whip the rest of the wedding details into shape. We've talked about that useful maxim "it takes a village," and now is the time to gather all of your villagers—bridesmaids, grandmothers, even flower girls. Everyone will have fun pitching in and bringing this rustic wedding vision to life, but don't wait too long to ask them!

Double Check the Details

» INDOOR AND OUTDOOR LIGHTING
» PARKING
» RESTROOMS
» INSURANCE
» CATERING AND BAR SETUP
» MUSIC SETUP
» ARRIVAL TIME FOR THE BRIDAL PARTY
» LENGTH OF THE RECEPTION (HOW LONG CAN YOU PARTY?)
» EXPECTED CLEANUP

PROJECTS & DÉCOR

Start by checking on the progress of any DIY projects to be certain they will be finished in time. Apply any final flourishes. Spruce up your flea market or secondhand finds. Glass bottles and Mason jars may need to be rinsed and cleaned. Paint may need to be touched up. Retrofit repurposed items for their new jobs if necessary.

Assemble anything that needs to be done in large quantities as far in advance as possible. Things like favors, seating assignments and welcome boxes can take a long time to put together—longer than you may anticipate, so get these out of the way early. If it's fresh-baked cookies or something fragile that needs to be done on-site, have a dependable crew at the ready to complete the task.

Think about all the jobs that may need to be done at the venue, and put together the ultimate wedding day toolbox. Be sure one trusted soul is in charge of the toolbox at all times.

Maggie's Tip

One quick trip to the store can help you collect all the goodies you will need for a wedding day toolbox. Make one filled with serious items needed such as the ones listed at right and then create a second one filled with fun items for the bride and bridesmaids to enjoy the day of the wedding, such as:

» MINI CHAMPAGNE BOTTLES
» BREATH MINTS
» SNACKS
» LIP GLOSS
» COOKIES
» WATER

Toolbox Supplies

» Scissors
» Tape
» Sewing kit
» Safety pins
» Flashlight
» Ribbon
» Glue

"Flea markets can be fun for all ages. Unsure how to get the family involved? My little trick: make a game of it. Think of something you need or an item that might be fun to find. Every time I go out with my nieces or nephews, we see how many cow creamers we can find. While I am searching for vintage items . . . , they are looking for a creative item too. The hunt can be entertaining for everyone!"
—LAUREN KRETER, BORROWED: A VINTAGE INSPIRED COMPANY

* The Flowers *

If you're handling the flowers yourself, you can't prepare the arrangements very far in advance without risking the integrity of the blooms. You can, however, get the other aspects in order so that when the time is right, all you have to do is add them in.

Have your assembly line worked out and a large enough workspace to accommodate everyone. Make up a few vases or centerpieces in advance so you know how long each one takes to put together. Be sure everyone knows what the finished product should look like, and have enough of the right tools on hand for everyone to maximize your team's efficiency.

Once finished, the floral arrangements will need to be transported to the venue and arrive looking good. Even if they are assembled on-site, they still need to be moved to the tables, ceremony sites and reception areas. Bring boxes, crates, wagons or wheelbarrows that can help get the job done quickly. Flowers need to stay as cool as possible, too, so if you are assembling the flowers yourself, locate a cooler to store them in until they're ready to be displayed.

I LOVE FLOWERS AND THINK THEY ARE EASIER TO TAKE ON AS A WEDDING PROJECT THAN EXPECTED. WITH THE HELP OF FAMILY AND FRIENDS, MY WEDDING FLOWERS WERE A COMPLETE DIY PROJECT.

* *The Dress* *

The wedding dress is one of the prime focal points of this special event so you will want to make sure that it's in perfect shape for its debut. Hang your dress in a place where it will stay wrinkle free for the big day—high enough so that the entire dress, even the train, is completely off the floor.

When your wedding day arrives you will be very excited to finally don the dress, but don't put it on too early. Sitting down before the ceremony could wrinkle the delicate fabric, and you don't want to spend the entire day standing, no matter how much you like your bridal shoes.

Maggie's Tip

Here are a few of my favorite designers who make the perfect dresses for a rustic chic wedding:

» SARAH SEVEN
» CLAIRE PETTIBONE
» TEMPERLEY LONDON
» JENNY PACKHAM
» ELIZABETH DYE
» VERONICA SHEAFFER
» LEANNE MARSHALL

Don't forget that many department stores have a bridal section as well. Check out Saks Fifth Avenue, Nordstrom, Bloomingdale's and Neiman Marcus.

RAINY DAY WEDDING MUST-HAVES

Let's face it—the weather on your wedding day is just a game of chance. One way to avoid a major last-minute crisis is to stash a few of the following items at the venue. If it rains, you'll be ready.

* Umbrellas *

Whether you color coordinate them, choose a pattern or simply stick with classic black, having umbrellas as backup is a must. Your bridesmaids will thank you and so will your guests if you have a few extra on hand for them. One bride even told me she selected beautiful green umbrellas and placed them in buckets at the entrance to her backyard wedding just in case the sky opened up. You don't have to break the bank to offer umbrellas to your guests, either. The best thing to do is buy a large stash for your ceremony and reception locations. If Mother Nature takes over, then you've covered your bases, but if the sun stays shining, you may be able to return them unused.

* Wellies *

It would be difficult to provide wellies, or rain boots, for all your guests, but if the forecast looks stormy, buy some cute rain boots for your bridesmaids, your flower girl, your mother, your fiancé's mother, and, of course, a white pair for yourself. Wellies look completely adorable in photos and are easy to switch in and out of as you move from one location to another. Our favorite vendor for boots is Hunter, but you can find more budget-friendly boots at Target and other big box stores. See more ideas for rain boots at a wedding on the Rustic Wedding Chic blog.

* Hay *

Hay can be a last-minute savior for a wedding hit by rain. Adding a layer of hay to an outdoor location like a backyard wedding or a backyard rehearsal dinner can soak up the water and help to prevent mud from forming. You can't exactly break out the hay if the rain comes unannounced, but it is something to consider doing in the days before the wedding if the weather is looking unreliable.

✴ Tarps ✴

For a very reasonable price you can get large clear-plastic tarps to protect items out in the open, including the ceremony chairs, floral arrangements, aisle runner and just about anything else that might get wet. This hardware store find is really useful at backyard weddings or anywhere you don't have a full venue staff to help.

"One of the wonderful and nerve-wracking things about throwing an outdoor wedding is the weather—the one thing you can't control! Instead, embrace it—plan for fun, rainy-day accessories (a great vintage umbrella or cute galoshes) that will look adorable and stylish in photos." —Amanda from Orchard Cove Photography

GUESTS SIT AT A TRULY RUSTIC LOCATION FOR THE START OF A
BREATHTAKING RUSTIC WEDDING CEREMONY.

OUTDOOR WEDDING MUST-HAVES

So many rustic weddings take place outdoors or in a venue like a barn with open sides. Consider having a few of the following items on hand to keep everyone comfortable.

* Bug Spray *

Unfortunately, mosquitos don't care if it's your wedding day. Keep bug spray handy so guests can focus on their dance moves well after the sun goes down and the bugs come out. You can even purchase convenient bug-repellant wipes for easy, mess-free application.

* Sunblock *

A farm-style wedding in the summer is wonderful, but, even if you are lucky enough to have cooperative weather, you may still be dealing with intense sun. Offer guests suntan lotion in a welcome bag so they don't take home sunburns along with their wedding favors.

* Fans *

Keeping guests cool at your wedding ceremony is a must—you don't want anyone overwhelmed by sun and heat. Place a fan on each of the seats at the ceremony so guests can watch you say "I do" in comfort. Fans are available in paper, straw and even bamboo to give you plenty of options to fit your wedding style.

* Water *

No doubt about it, having water available for your guests is a must—the more abundant, the better. Offer pre-ceremony bottled water and Mason jars of ice water during cocktail hour to keep everyone happy and hydrated.

YOUR TEAM

So many rustic venues, while picturesque and charming, don't always come with a full-service staff. Designate a team for setup, cleanup and collection of all the decorations and supplies. Helpful friends and family members can gather the twinkle lights or take out trash the next morning. Remember, many hands make light work! By enlisting a group, you will not only achieve your goals of a beautiful, flawless wedding, you will have created a community of people who helped make the day a success. And what could be more beautiful than that?

Jobs that Need a Point Person

» ARRANGING ESCORT CARDS / PLACE CARDS
» HANDING OUT PROGRAMS
» DISPLAYING FAVORS
» DELIVERING WELCOME BAGS
» PLACING WEDDING SIGNS
» CEREMONY BACKDROP

* NOTES & RESOURCES *

Crafting an ongoing list of wedding resources is an essential part of making sure you have the best for your wedding day. From where to shop to photographers, keeping a list of vendors and resources for your wedding will ensure that each and every detail for your wedding is executed perfectly.

ONLINE RESOURCES

ETSY: Etsy.com

LOVERLY: Lover.ly

PINTEREST: Pinterest.com/rusticwedchic

RUSTIC WEDDING CHIC: RusticWeddingChic.com

RUSTIC WEDDING GUIDE: RusticWeddingGuide.com

INVITATIONS & PAPER

AUGUST PARK CREATIVE: Augustpark.com

THE BLUE ENVELOPE: The-blue-envelope.com

LOVE VS. DESIGN: Lovevsdesign.com

MINTED: Minted.com

PAIGE SIMPLE STUDIO: Paigesimple.com

PAPERLESS POST: PaperlessPost.com

STEEL PETAL PRESS: Steelpetalpress.com

WEDDING PAPER DIVAS: WeddingPaperDivas.com

CRAFTS

AC MOORE: Nationwide

CREATE FOR LESS: CreateForLess.com

HOBBY LOBBY: Nationwide

JOANNE FABRIC & CRAFT STORE: Nationwide

MICHAEL'S CRAFT STORE: Nationwide

SAVE ON CRAFTS: Save-on-Crafts.com

SPECIALTY STORES

HIHO HOME MARKET: Gardiner, NY

HOMEGOODS: Nationwide

IKEA: Nationwide

TARGET: Nationwide

FASHION

ANTHROPOLOGIE: Anthropologie.com

BELLA BRIDESMAID: Bellabridesmaid.com

BETSY WISE BRIDAL: Betsywisebridal.com

BHLDN: bhldn.com

BLOOMINGDALE'S: Bloomingdales.com

CLAIRE PETTIBONE: Clairepettibone.com

ELIZABETH DYE: Elizabethdye.com

EVERTHINE BRIDAL BOUTIQUE: Shopeverthine.com

FANCY BRIDAL: Fancybridalny.com

HUNTER: USA.hunter-boot.com

IVY & ASTER: Ivyandaster.com

J.CREW: Jcrew.com

JENNY PACKHAM: Jennypackham.com

LEANNE MARSHALL: Leanimal.com

MODCLOTH: Modcloth.com

NEIMAN MARCUS: Neimanmarcus.com

NORDSTROM: Nordstrom.com

SARAH SEVEN: Sarahseven.com

TEMPERLEY LONDON: Temperleylondon.com

VERONICA SHEAFFER: Vsgowns.com

BOOKS

Barn Weddings, MAGGIE LORD, GIBBS SMITH BOOKS

Handmade Weddings, EUNICE MOYLE, SABRINA MOYLE AND SHANA FAUST, CHRONICLE BOOKS

Mason Jar Crafts, LAUREN ELISE DONALDSON, ULYSSES PRESS

Rustic Wedding Chic, MAGGIE LORD, GIBBS SMITH BOOKS

FLEA MARKETS

If you are looking for one-of-a-kind decorations, vintage treasures, repurposed items or just about anything else, you might want to consider heading out to your local flea market. Below are a few of the most respected flea markets across the country.

ALAMEDA POINT ANTIQUE FAIRE, ALAMEDA, CA: AlamedaPointAntiquesFaire.com

BRIMFIELD, BRIMFIELD, MA: BrimfieldShow.com

BROOKLYN FLEA, BROOKLYN, NY: BrooklynFlea.com

CHICAGO ANTIQUE MARKET, CHICAGO, IL: RandolphStreetMarket.com

THE ELEPHANT'S TRUNK, NEW MILFORD, CT: ETFlea.com

FIRST MONDAY TRADE DAYS, CANTON, TX: FirstMondayCanton.com

FREMONT SUNDAY STREET MARKET, SEATTLE, WA: FremontMarket.com

RALEIGH FLEA MARKET, RALEIGH, NC: RaleighFleaMarket.net

THE ROSE BOWL FLEA MARKET, PASADENA, CA: RGCShows.com

SCOTT ANTIQUE MARKET, ATLANTA, GA: ScottAntiqueMarket.com

SPRINGFIELD ANTIQUE SHOW & FLEA MARKET, SPRINGFIELD, OH: SpringfieldAntiqueShow.com

VENDORS WE LOVE

Having your wedding go off without a hitch usually is dependent on selecting just the right vendors. From talented event planners to masterful photographers, vendors play an important role in your wedding. We know better than anyone how many thousands of gifted wedding vendors are out there, but below are a few that we feel are some of the best. For a complete list of rustic wedding vendors, please visit RusticWeddingGuide.com.

PHOTOGRAPHERS

EE Photography: EePhotoMe.com

Jean Kallina Photography: JeanKallinaPhotography.com

Jennifer Bakos: JennBakosPhoto.com

Joyeuse Photography: JoyeusePhotography.com

Maggie Carson Romano: MCR-Weddings.com

Orchard Cove Photography: OrchardCovePhotography.com

Siegel Thurston Photography: SiegelThurston.com

Shannon Confair Photography: ShannonConfairPhotography.com

EVENT PLANNERS

Ashlie Virginia Events: AshleeVirginiaEvents.com

Balboa Weddings & Events: Balboaweddings.com

Forget-Me-Not Events: 4getmenotevents.com

Gold Leaf Event Design & Production: Goldleafevent.com

Rambling House Events & Food Design: RamblingHouseEvents.com

RENTALS

Borrowed: A Vintage Inspired Company: Borrowedvintagestyle.com

Chicago Vintage Weddings: ChicagoVintageWeddings.com

Found Vintage Rentals: Foundrentals.com

HiHo Home Market: HihoHome.com

Little Vintage Rentals: LittleVintageRentals.com

Miss Match Rentals: MissMatchRentals.com

Mrs. Vintage: MrsVintageRentals.com

Rent My Dust Rentals: RentMyDust.com

Swoon Vintage Rental Co: SwoonVintageRentalCo.com

Vintage Charlotte: Vintage-Charlotte.com

PHOTOGRAPHY CREDITS

Bamber Photography: Bamberphotography.net 18–20, 82

EE Photography: 8; 12; 16 top right, middle; 24; 26 top; 32; 36–37; 39 bottom; 48–49; 50; 54 bottom; 76 left; 77 top, bottom right; 83; 144–145; 150; 156 middle left, middle right, bottom left

Jean Kallina Photography: jacket, back cover, middle left; 22; 29 bottom; 31 bottom left; 44–45; 79; 146

Jennifer Bakos: Jennbakosphoto.com jacket, back cover, top left; 7: 23; 29 top; 38; 39 top; 153; 155 left

Shannon Confair Photography: jacket, back cover, top right; 16 bottom left; 31 bottom right; 46; 156 top right

Siegel Thurston Photography: Siegelthurston. com 1, 15, 26 bottom, 33, 42, 70 bottom right, 76 right, 77 bottom left, 149 top, 155 right, 160

Tahni Candelaria of Joyeuse Photography: 4–5; 10; 16 top left, bottom right; 31 top; 41; 70 bottom left; 156 top left, bottom right